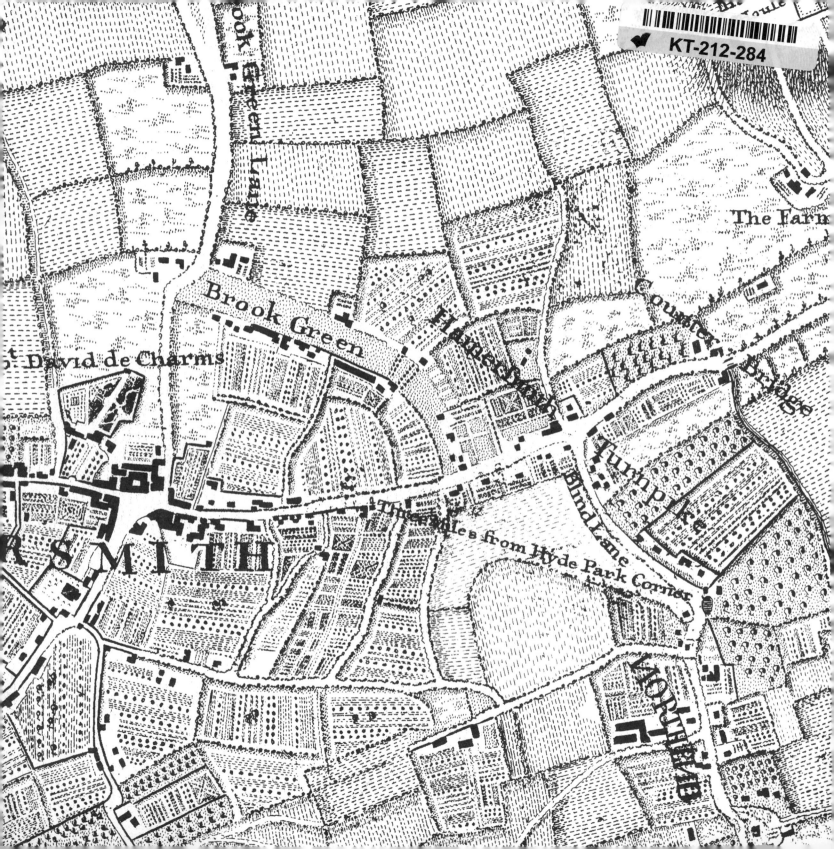

WILD ABOUT
Hammersmith
& Brook Green

THE TALE OF TWO WEST LONDON VILLAGES

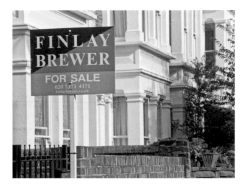

Finlay Brewer has been wild about Hammersmith & Brook Green since we opened our first branch in Blythe Road in 1992 and over 20 years later we still feel the same way. We may have expanded our horizons West to include W12 and W3, but our belief, confidence in and love of W14 and W6 remains at the core of our business.

As the leading independent estate agent in the area for both sales and lettings, we know the schools, the pubs, the restaurants, the myriad transport links and, most importantly, we know the people who live here, many as friends. Being part of the community and supporting that community is a role we take very seriously which is why we support local events like Brook Green Day and local charities including the Hammersmith Community Gardens Association on an on-going basis.

Sponsoring this wonderful book gives us the opportunity to share our affection for this special part of West London and through Andrew Wilson's eyes we could not have wished for a more evocative and diverse visual celebration of our neighbourhood.

We hope you enjoy this book as much as we have enjoyed being a part of its creation and that you will continue to help us promote Hammersmith & Brook Green as a delightful place to call home.

138 Shepherds Bush Road London W6 7PB
020 7371 4171   info@finlaybrewer.co.uk   www.finlaybrewer.co.uk

Clockwise from top left: autumn colours for sale, Holy Trinity Brook Green, outside the boat houses on the Lower Mall, Brook Green Hotel.

Contents

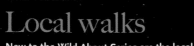

NEW FEATURE

Local walks

New to the Wild About Series are the local walks allowing you to really get to know the area as depicted in each book. *(See page 190)*

Welcome to Wild About Hammersmith & Brook Green

Hammersmith and Brook Green lie just a short skip and a jump from where I live on the other side of the river in Putney, so I was really pleased when my friends at Finlay Brewer suggested that I might like to come 'North' and cast my camera over their green and pleasant patch. Being so close, I was already very familiar with the area, especially the fabulous bridge but having the perfect excuse to take my wanderings further was just brilliant. My children went to school here, so I have very fond memories of the walks to school and it was fun retracing my steps.

What made these journeys that bit better was being introduced early on to my historian Caroline, as she was able to place all these wonderful sights into their proper context. She was also the perfect partner for my new idea of adding some walks to my books, since besides being a writer she is also a guide. So once you have experienced this lovely area of west London from the comfort of your armchair you can then sample the delights for yourself, beautifully devised by Caroline.

As followers of my work will know I love my open spaces and the Hammersmith area has an array of beauties, some better known than others. In between, there are distinct communities, delightful little streets and then the river, of course. The last 18 months have been great fun and I hope you enjoy my photographic journey.

As with all my books, there are many people who come together to make the whole thing possible. Firstly, there are my sponsors, local estate agent Finlay Brewer, garden company Shoots and Leaves and lighting company Holloways of Ludlow. Any help is welcome but these guys went that bit further for which I am exceedingly grateful. I would also like to thank my writer Caroline MacMillan, who not only provided my introduction but also many of the extended captions found throughout the book. Do take a look at her walks, and perhaps even meet her, as I'm sure she'd love to accompany you around the area. There is also my graduate intern from Roehampton University, Jessica Dean, who joined me towards the end of this project and who was a fantastic help in those last frantic weeks. Thank you also to local artist Pauline Morrison for providing a lovely map of the area. Then there is my designer, Tim Ball and colour expert, Paul Sherfield, who help ensure that all this work is not in vain and looks fabulous on the page.

My books take well over a year to produce and I meet many people along the way who have helped or contributed and unfortunately space does not allow me to mention you all. As much as possible I try to reference people in relevant editorial within the book but please forgive me if I have inadvertently missed you out, it's nothing personal. With such a rich canvas to work from but only so much time, there are also several places that might feel short changed; again, my apologies.

Being a visitor to your town in the last 18 months has been a delight and I hope you enjoy my travelogue as much as I enjoyed making it.

Andrew Wilson, October 2014

Left: Josie, my springer spaniel and constant companion, underneath the railway bridge in Ravenscourt Park.

Sunset on Hammersmith Bridge

Hammersmith & Brook Green

A SHORT HISTORY OF THE AREAS
by Caroline MacMillan

Archaeological fragments unearthed during the building of Hammersmith Bridge in 1825 indicate a second century Roman settlement had existed at this part of the Thames, but it was many years before a hamlet established itself on the willowy banks of the slow moving river. In the 11th century, the Domesday Book records a small settlement near today's Furnivall Gardens where a tributary of what came to be called Stamford Brook flowed into the Thames.

The first record of the name Hammersmyth appears in 1294, the name possibly derived from a combination of the Old English words of Hamor (a hammer) and Smyththe (smithy). The land was part of the Manor of Fulham, owned by the Bishop of London whose country palace lay downstream at Putney. The original topography featured heavily forested land, which provided acorns and beechnuts to feed pigs whilst the river was a valuable source of food including eels, salmon and wild fowl as well as providing a means of transport to the City of London.

By the 17th century the forests were being cleared for farmland and the thousand inhabitants included some wealthy merchants such as The Earl of Mulgrave, a veteran of the Spanish Armada, who owned the Butterwick Estate on which the Hammersmith Broadway Bus Station now sits. Crisp Road was owned by Sir Nicholas Crisp, now the location of Riverside Studios. A loyal supporter of King Charles I, Crisp built his country house on the bend in the river "in sweet and wholesome air".

Until the consecration in 1631 of a chapel-of-ease near Hammersmith Creek which ran from the east end of King Street to the river, residents had a long muddy walk to Fulham parish church in Putney. By 1883, at the height of churchgoing, the chapel dedicated to St Paul was replaced by the larger church which now sits adjacent to the A4 flyover, marooned in a sea of busy roads. There was a strong Catholic presence in the area following the decision of Queen Catherine of Braganza, Charles II's Portuguese widow, to build a country house in Hammersmith. By 1677 Quakers had their Meeting House near Hammersmith Creek and in 1875 Methodists found a permanent home in their King Street church whilst Rev. William Booth, founder of The Salvation Army and a resident of Ravenscourt Road, established a Christian Mission in Dalling Road.

During the 19th century a considerable amount of farmland was turned over to the creation of brickfields as the clay soil provided good building materials for London as it continued to expand westwards. Many ponds and lakes were formed as a result of this activity and

Riverside Studios built on the land originally owned by Sir Nicholas Crisp, a loyal supporter of King Charles I.

Lakeside Road near Brook Green is a reminder of this extremely profitable business. Nearer to the river, the good soil enabled farmers to grow soft fruits such as gooseberries, redcurrants, raspberries and strawberries, which were taken by boat or carried in panniers made by osiers from riverside willows to sell at Covent Garden market.

Hammersmith is renowned for its fantastic schools. Edward Latymer's bequest of 1642 enabled a boys' school to be founded which still bears his name. He later provided additional funds to amalgamate with Sir William Godolphin's 17th century school to form Godolphin & Latymer. St Paul's Boys' School moved from the City's cathedral to healthier Hammersmith in 1884 occupying buildings designed by Alfred Waterhouse until the school decamped again in 1968 across the river to Barnes. During the Second World War, Waterhouse's buildings were the headquarters of the 21st Army Group under the command of former pupil, General Bernard Montgomery. St Paul's Girls' School, founded by the Mercers, opened in 1904 and has had several distinguished directors of music including Herbert Howells and Gustav Holst, the latter composing his St Paul's and Brook Green suites for his pupils.

King Street, once known as the King's Highway, formed part of the main route from London to Windsor and The Swan on the Broadway was a popular booking house for stage coaches. One notable example of the many taverns along King Street was the Hampshire Hog, which in 1741 stood in half an acre of ground and had its own stabling and butchers shop. Initially independent bakers, butchers and grocers shops served the local population but by the 1930s King Street had expanded to include Palmer's Department Store, Marks & Spencer, Boots and Woolworths some of which still remain

Top: This stone marks the location of the old Dove's Press next to the Dove pub (page 76).

Middle: A plaque commemorates the spot where Lieutenant Charles Campbell saved the life of a woman but lost his own (page 14).

Bottom: St Paul's Girls School named their music building after their famous music teacher Gustav Holst.

and exist alongside a shopping mall and other major chains including H&M, TKMaxx and Primark.

The lure of the riverside attracted a wonderful variety of residents including J.M.W. Turner who established a summer house and studio near the Old Ship; it was whilst he lived here in 1811 that he submitted 'Apollo and the Python' to the Royal Academy. William Morris lived at Kelmscott House and described the location as being "certainly the prettiest in London". As well as being an influential writer and designer of fabrics and wall

papers he was a founding member, together with Karl Marx's daughter, of the Hammersmith branch of the Socialist League. The writer and humourist, A.P. Herbert, who served as MP for the University of Oxford for 15 years, delighted in travelling in his boat, The Water Gypsy, from his home in Hammersmith Terrace to the House of Commons.

The opening of the Metropolitan line from Paddington to Hammersmith in 1864, followed seven years later by the District Line, made the area very attractive to those seeking work in the City and between 1881

and 1901 the population soared from 72,000 to 112,000. This growth triggered an explosion in residential expansion and the market gardens disappeared under terraces of houses. Businesses flourished too, including builders merchant Sankey who unloaded materials at their wharf at Hammersmith Creek until the 1920s when it was filled in. The Town Hall now acts as a marker to its location. George Wimpey opened his stonemason's yard in Hammersmith Grove in 1896 and the company's headquarters remained there for over a hundred years.

During the First World War, the local Home Guard dug trenches in Ravenscourt Park and held band practice under the railway arches, whilst during the Second World War Belgian refugees from Dunkirk were accommodated at Upper Latymer School. Hammersmith did not escape the bombs and at the height of the Blitz, the King and Queen visited areas stricken by the assault. After the King's death, the Queen Mother kept her promise and returned to see the opening of the Spring Vale Estate.

One of the biggest changes to the face of Hammersmith was the opening of the A4 flyover in 1961 and the development of the Broadway itself which saw the last Victorian shop terraces swept away and replaced with glazed office blocks, apart from the facade of Bradmore House. In the 1980s The Ark, an innovative office building which resembles an ocean liner, rose beside the flyover and in recent years Lyric Square has been revitalized and the flourishing weekly market stalls act a vibrant reminder of Hammersmith's village past.

Caroline MacMillan, 2014

Top: The Spring Vale Estate, opened by Queen Elizabeth The Queen Mother.

Left: The Hampshire Hog, which in 1741 stood in half an acre of ground and had its own stabling and butcher's shop.

I n 1493, the first mention of Brook Green appears in a document referring to a probably manmade tributary of Stamford Brook, named Black Bull Ditch or Parr's Ditch, which flowed across the marshy green to enter the Thames south of Chancellor's Wharf. By the late 18th century this offshoot was charmingly recorded as being "a 4ft wide ditch, constantly full of filthy water" which eventually became so polluted with waste from nearby brick fields that it was finally covered and converted to a sewer in 1876. Nearby Blythe Road, known as Blinde Lane, was recorded in 1839 as being "sadly neglected and nearly impassable in winter".

During the 18th and early 19th century the area was primarily known for its market gardens, the most famous founded by James Lee and Lewis Kennedy on the site of a former vineyard; Olympia now marks the spot. Lee and Kennedy introduced hundreds of new plants to the United Kingdom, including standard roses and fuchsias, the latter discovered growing in a sailor's garden in Wapping having been brought back by him from Chile. During this era, a fair held on the Green was a popular annual event, but having attracted some undesirable characters it was closed by magistrate order in 1823.

Towards the end of the 18th century, the brickfields and market gardens were beginning to give way to some larger dwellings, including Eagle House situated on the corner of Luxemburg Gardens, with its grand entrance flanked by two impressive stone eagles. Demolished in the 1890s, Bute House now stands on its site. The Grange, to the east of Rowan Road, became the home of the famous Victorian actor Henry Irving and St Paul's Girls' School was built on part of its grounds. The original Blythe House stood north of the Green but had long since disappeared by the time the Post Office opened their Savings Bank and offices in a building of the same name in 1899. The Post Office workers have now gone, but the stunning building remains as a store for the V&A, Science and British Museums.

For many years there was a strong Roman Catholic presence in the area to the extent that it was sometimes referred to as Pope's Corner. Eagle House was at one time occupied by the religious organisation of St Vincent and a school for girls known as "The Ark" was established in 1760 at Brook Green House to "save them from a deluge of vice". The Ark was taken over by the Catholic Poor Schools Committee in 1847 to be a teacher trainer college and remained there until 1925 when it moved to Strawberry Hill. In the mid 1900s, The Holy Trinity church served the influx of Irish workers whilst the fast growing west London Jewish community built a synagogue on the north side of the Green.

The latter struggled with attendance and eventually closed before finally becoming home to the Chinese Christian Church in London.

During the 19th century, laundries abounded in the area, including on the site now occupied by Berghem Mews, and an 80 foot chimney towered over McCullock's bleaching grounds in Spring Vale where calico and muslins were whitened and starched. In 1873 Charles Cadby, a piano manufacturer, demolished two houses facing Hammersmith Road to build a new factory, a site that was latterly bought by Joseph Lyons in 1899 which expanded over the next ninety years to become a vast food manufacturing complex employing over 30,000 workers. One of these workers was a young research chemist called Margaret Thatcher who helped develop ways of preserving ice cream – so that's where she developed that famous frosty look!

Above: The Blue Plaque on Brook Green for Silver Studios.

Below: A plaque quoting William Morris above the William Morris Museum.

Brook Green attracted a number of talented artists and the blue plaque at 84 Brook Green remembers the Silver Studios, whose designs were sold to leading fabric and wallpaper manufacturers including Sanderson and Liberty's. Sir Frank Short, the eminent engraver, lived at number 56 whilst on the other side of the Green another blue plaque records Gustav Holst's time as Director of Music at St Paul's Girls' School.

Now a conservation area, Brook Green and its surrounding roads are largely residential with houses which command rather higher prices than in 1855, when a semi-detached seven room cottage on the Green could be rented for a mere £25 a year. Plans in the 1930s to build a new town hall on the Green were seen off by irate residents who ensured that Brook Green's much valued open space was preserved to be enjoyed for many years to come.

Caroline MacMillan, 2014

Hammersmith is blessed with a number of societies and residents groups whose members include architects, historians, artists, engineers and town planners who devote – on a strictly voluntary basis – thousands of hours annually to researching, recording, preserving, enhancing and promoting the historic buildings and gardens of its riverside community. These include:

The Hammersmith Society
www.hammersmithsociety.org.uk;

Hammersmith Mall Residents Association
www.hamra.org.uk;

The Hammersmith and Fulham Historic Buildings Group
www.hfhbg.org.uk;

Friends of Furnivall Gardens
www.londongardensonline.org.uk/gardens;

The West London River Group
www.wlrg.org.uk;

Friends of Brook Green
www.friendsofbrookgreen.org.uk.

Hammersmith & Brook Green

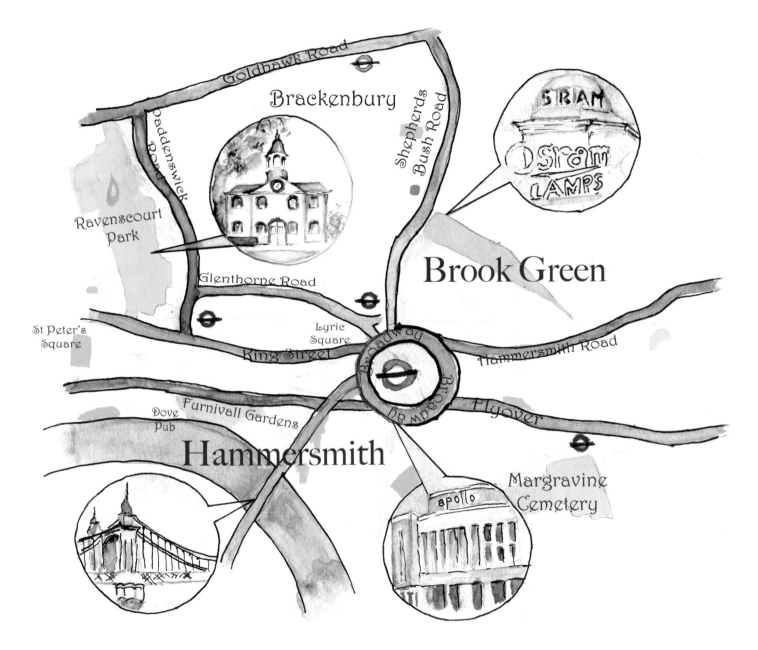

This map was kindly supplied by local artist, Pauline Morrison and is not meant to be absolutely to scale but to give the reader a fun introduction to the area and some of the places covered in this book. Pauline lives and works in Battersea and specialises in watercolours. She can be contacted via her website *www.sofap.co.uk/paulinemorrison.html*

Hammersmith Bridge

The Hammersmith Bridge we see today is not the original crossing. Regular users of the bridge will be no stranger to the frequent road works and refurbishments on the crossing, a tradition that the original bridge began. First built in 1827, the first bridge was a toll bridge, and similar in design, though missing the recognisable spires on the suspension towers. It was demolished in 1884 as it could no longer support the weight of the travellers crossing the river and in 1887, the present Hammersmith Bridge was opened by the Prince of Wales. The IRA almost demolished it in 1939 but the quick thinking of Maurice Childs, who threw the bomb into the water, saved the bridge; he was awarded an MBE for his bravery. This was not the only courageous act on the bridge in the 20th Century; in 1919 Lieutenant Charles Campbell Wood, a South African serving in the Royal Air Force, jumped in the Thames to save a woman from drowning, though later died from his injuries. A plaque commemorates his heroism on the bridge (page 7).

Tierney Clark, designer of the 1824 bridge also built the first bridge to link Buda and Pest in Hungary. His brief was to design a "bridge of suspension with a view to the strictest economy" and during excavations the remains of a Roman sword was found in the mud giving an indication of an early settlement in the area.

Originally painted "with a pink coat", it turned green in 1888 and grey during war years. It was restored to its former green and gold glory in 1986.

Opposite: Any Londoner knows that the weather can change quickly in the city, but rarely did it look as dramatic as it did here early one morning in March 2014 on Hammersmith Bridge, as a heavy fog was lifting.

Bottom: Crowds literally hanging off the bridge to watch the Boat Race. Courtesy of Maisie Brown.

Hammersmith Bridge marks the beginning of Lower Mall on the river. From here you can see big waves caused by boats going underneath the bridge, usually free to move even when the traffic above is crawling at a snails pace.

It's fair to say that the traffic can sometimes be bad on the bridge but there is a reason for this; they try to limit as best they can the flow on the bridge itself to try and limit the weight.

Occasionally, however, boats have been known to get stuck at high tide, unable to get under the low bridge.

These Hammersmith based offices and houses are blessed with beautiful views across the Thames to Barnes. At low tide it is possible to walk on the foreshore.

In 1933 the Triumph Film Company moved into Riverside Studios on the Thames, the large white building beside the bridge. Episodes of Father Brown, Hancock's Half Hour and early episodes of Doctor Who were recorded here until the 1970s. More recently Channel 4 have been using it for shows like T4. It is now up for re-development, which caused some local people to object due to its scale. However, the developers do intend to re-open the Studios and provide other amenities. They also plan to include a new walkway, which will stop people having to go around to get back to the river.

Hammersmith Bridge is a wonderful place to view some stunning sunsets.

Thank you to Susan and Michael, who both live in Digby Mansions for the offer of viewing the river from their homes (their apartments are on the North West corner of the bridge with the rather attractive green dome), we never quite got it together but thank you all the same and I hope you enjoy what I did succeed in capturing.

Looking west towards
Hammersmith from the bank
on the Barnes side of the river.
Fully repaired after the IRA
bomb in 2000, the bridge still
carries a weight restriction and
barriers at either end to limit
the traffic on the bridge.

The Boat Race

Hammersmith Bridge has been a favourite vantage point to view the Boat Race (see page 16 for a shot from the 19th century). In 1870 over 11,000 people crowded onto the bridge to cheer Oxford and Cambridge University crews as they rowed from Putney to Mortlake. Today thousands line the banks of the river whilst millions more watch the race on television. The tradition was started by two childhood friends, Charles Merivale of Cambridge, and Charles Wordsworth of Oxford, a race which Oxford won, apparently with ease.

These races can be dangerous, as seen in the 2012 event. A protester swam into the course, halting proceedings, and after the race was restarted, such effort was applied that one of Oxford's bowman had to receive emergency treatment at the end of the race after fainting from exhaustion. In 2014, there was a coming together of oars prior to reaching Hammersmith Bridge, with Oxford the beneficiary, who eventually went onto win the race.

Brook Green

The area of Brook Green connects Hammersmith to its neighbouring towns of Kensingston, Shepherds Bush and Holland Park, and is one of the more up market areas of Hammersmith, described by *The Times* as the "New French Quarter". Named after the Brook Green park, it is one of the most picturesque places to live and work in the area. It was originally built as an industrialisation expansion of London and was home to the J. Lyons factory, a restaurant chain, and the Osram light bulb factory. The beautiful architecture of the time has remained, but has lost the busy industrial nature in favour of a tight knit community. Formally stretching along the Stamford Brook, this waterway is now underground, part of it still beneath the Brook Green Hotel.

Opposite: The Brook Green Hotel has stood at the west end of the green since 1886, when it was used as a coach house for weary travelling Victorians.

Bottom: It was in 1893 that Mr. Robertson took over a brush making factory and founded the Osram and Robertson Lamp Company to produce electric lamp bulbs. The project was a success and evolved into the General Electric Company (GEC). The business eventually moved but Osram's distinctive original light bulb tower continues to shine out above the supermarket and Peabody residential estate which replaced the factory.

Top right: Praised by Nigella Lawson and frequented by Simon Cowell, Kerbisher & Malt on Shepherds Bush Road. Started in 2011, they aim to make fish and chips simple, fresh and tasty. As one of the owner's was a fisherman, they named the ship after the old Kerbisher fishing boat.

Thanks to Hind, the manageress, for posing so beautifully, plus the photobomber behind her and her colleague in the doorway – clearly a fun place.

The playground cost £200,000 to build, and was created through the hard work of fundraising projects and events like Brook Green Day every September. Facilities such as these in the area keep it beautifully enclosed and promotes the community atmosphere that is so strong in this area of Hammersmith.

Brook Green used to be a marshy wasteland before it was industrialised, but those days are long gone. From 1800 an annual fair was held on Brook Green, but was stopped in 1823 due to fears that the raucous entertainment would corrupt the youth. Today, the Friends of Brook Green throw a fair in the park.

This page: Brook Green Fair is organised every summer by the Friends of Brook Green.

For up to date news on their activities and to find out about membership please visit *www. friendsofbrookgreen.org*

Christmas Trees on Brook Green

Shoots & Leaves, selling their particular brand of Christmas trees has been a familiar sight on Brook Green opposite the Hotel since 2000. Based locally, they go to extraordinary lengths to source the best trees, they now sell over 5,000 a year and will even deliver and put it up for you.

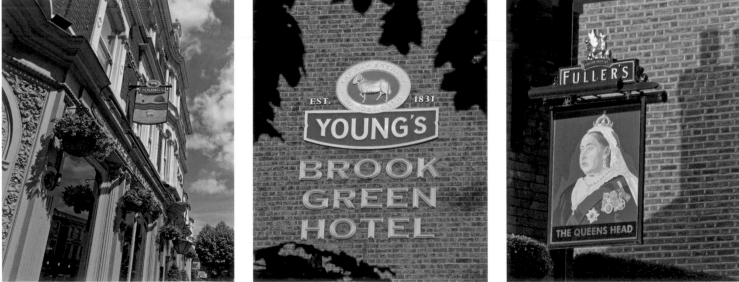

Opposite: Because of the road that ran through the town on its way out of the city, Hammersmith was a wonderful target for highwaymen. Dick Turpin himself frequented the Queen's Head pub, stealing from the rich and spending it at the pub. Brook Green Hotel opened in 1884 on the west side of Brook Green and has remained open ever since.

Top right: The terrace houses that run along the north side of the green visibly change as you walk. The first houses to be built were those at the far east of the green, built for Irish labourers, an area that was called a 'rookery' by the Kensington Gazette. The area improved as more houses were built, leading to the beautiful avenues we see today.

Bottom right: Ecole Française de Londres, a French school, is situated next to the green.

Bottom left: A blue plaque commemorates the Silver Studios that was established here in 1880. Integral in the development of British Art Noveau, this company designed patterned wallpapers that were mass produced and decorated the homes of many.

Street Scenes

Hammersmith's streets are a combination of modern city additions and alterations, and the older houses, buildings and structures which date back centuries. It is easy to turn a corner and find yourself transported back to the 1800s, only to be met five minutes later with the modern glass based Bus and Train station and the modern office blocks around the busy Hammersmith Broadway. The flyover, built in 1961, which is currently under extensive repair, was used in the Ride London cycle race (see page 54), and many locals came out on the Sunday of the now annual event to watch over 20,000 cyclists as they made their way past.

At Hammersmith's centre, King Street runs from Hammersmith Bus Station all the way to Ravenscourt Park before it turns into Chiswick High Road. Most of the area's shops trail along the road, displaying, like the rest of the town, a blend of old and new architecture. Brook Green and Brackenbury Village's residential roads have some of the most sought after houses in London, with beautiful common areas and big living spaces. One of the first areas you encounter when leaving the station on The Broadway is Lyric Square, an engraved paving slab boasting that William Morris once spoke on that spot, just across from the Lyric Theatre. King Street is also home to Hammersmith's last remaining cinema, Cineworld, a converted cinema from the art deco period, evident from its curved façade. Just a little further west, as trees start to adorn the pavements, the massive Premier Inn stands tall and glassy, right next door to the Palingswick House.

Many churches can be found throughout the town, such as the beautiful St Peter's church in St Peter's Square, St Paul's Church, and the local Salvation Army branch is housed in a particularly fine building (see page 100). And for all you sinners, there are still plenty of pubs, both old and new.

Hammersmith Broadway

On a warm day, St Paul's Churchyard is a perfect location for a picnic, as it's the closest green space to the bus station and the centre of the town. The wagtails have become so tame that they will come and feed from your hand.

Above: The Hammersmith Surgery on Bridge Road has a sleek, curved facade that almost won it the Stirling Prize for excellence in architecture in 2001.

Top: St Paul's church peers over the bus station, overlooking the town with an all seeing eye. Despite the proliferation of tall buildings, the church can still be seen from all around.

Bottom: The Ark was created by Swedish architect Ralph Erskine in 1992, and named for the boat like exterior. While it has changed hands a few times, and been extensively renovated inside, it still remains a fascinating piece of local architecture, dominating the skyline as you approach Hammersmith along the A4.

When the Gaumont cinema first opened in 1932 it was described as the last word in modern architecture. During the years when it was the Hammersmith Odeon locals fondly referred to it as 'Hammy O'. Audience members travel from far and wide to attend events at the Hammersmith Apollo, and so do the performers; in 2014 Kate Bush did a completely sold out two month series of shows in the venue. The splendid Art Deco interior is well preserved and admired by those attending live musical and comedy evenings, and the original refurbished Compton Organ can be once again played, a hark back to the building's origins in 1932.

Completed in 1961, the Hammersmith Flyover was built to carry the ever increasing volume of traffic over Hammersmith rather than through its clogged up gyratory system; it was one of the first elevated roads to use reinforced concrete. The heated cables to eliminate ice formation were initially very successful until a huge electricity bill during the winter so shocked Hammersmith council that they cut off the supply completely. A recent proposal for a 'flyunder' tunnel has yet to be agreed but would certainly give Hammersmith residents easier access to their river frontage. As we publish this, the Flyover is undergoing extensive strengthening work, due to complete in summer 2015.

To celebrate the 150th anniversary of the Hammersmith and City tube line, TFL brought a steam train and two buses from their museum for the commuters to enjoy. You could then travel on the train, which travelled between Moorgate and Hammersmith all day. Actors and a brass band entertained the customers on their route. The Hammersmith and City line was the second tube line to be built, after the Metropolitan.

This page: With todays modern architecture, there is a lot of glass, and Hammersmith has its fair share. Far left, St Paul's church is reflected in the office block in front of Marks and Spencer. Top right, the office building at number 10 Hammersmith Grove and bottom, the building in Shortlands, next to the Novotel.

Opposite top left: This 18th century facade belongs to Bradmore House on the Broadway, formerly Smollensky's restaurant. The old 18th century facade was taken from the extension of the 16th century mansion, Butterwick House. This beautiful example of English Baroque domestic architecture was moved so that it faces west, and was elevated so that it could be used as a front for the garage that owned the site. As a Grade II listed building, it is one of the more architecturally significant buildings in the area.

Opposite top right: Rebuilt in 1901, the Swan Hotel on the corner of the Broadway and King Street was an important booking stage for coaches on their journey along King Street and onwards to the west of England.

Opposite bottom right: The West London Hospital was open from 1856 to 1993. It was built for the local community, though needs quickly changed when Britain went to war. When it eventually closed, Sony bought the building and now uses it as its offices.

Ride London

Ride London was started in 2013, a re-creation of the Olympic bike ride the previous year that had so impressed Boris Johnson, the Mayor of London. The route starts in Queen Elizabeth Olympic Park and goes all the way south to Leith Hill in Surrey, before turning north and back into London.

The Sunday of this weekend cycling celebration sees over 20,000 ameteur and 150 elite cyclists tackle an almost 200km route.

St Paul's Church

St Paul's church, now partially obscured by the A4 flyover, is on the site of a Chapel-of-Ease which was consecrated in 1630 and saved residents from the long and often muddy walk to the nearest church, All Saints, Fulham, by Putney Bridge.

The present building was designed by JP Seddon and HR Gough in 1883 and contains 17th and 18th century monuments from the previous chapel, which was demolished for being too small for the population and was considered an eyesore. This obviously isn't still the case; the new building looks beautiful whatever the season.

Lyric Square

For over a hundred years Lyric Square has been the venue for an open market. It was here that William Morris stood to recruit members to the Hammersmith Socialist League which he formed with Karl Marx's daughter.

During the summer of 2014, the local council ran an arts festival, fun for kids and adults alike, especially the water fountain, which is an all year feature. Demonstrating their juggling skills, and in the case of Charlie, stilts as

well, are 'Albert and Friends Instant Circus' who have been based in the area for 30 years. Thank you to the manager of the Hop Poles pub for allowing me to take a picture from their lounge window!

I am grateful to Lorraine from the council, who helps manage the market, for introducing me to some of the vendors. The Square now hosts a regular farmers' market on a Thursday with a World Food Market on Friday, where the local community and office workers alike can sample Caribbean style salads, Thai cuisine curries, crêpes and ever popular falafels as an alternative to a lunch time sandwich.

Top left: Sibylle from Olivier's Bakery.

Top right: Left is Barry Bloom from Bloom Kitchens and right is Jamie Rivera from Cheeky Burgers (bottom right).

Opening in 1895 the Lyric Theatre, splendidly designed by Frank Matcham, had a seating capacity of 775. In the 1970s disaster loomed as the surrounding area was earmarked for redevelopment but following a public campaign the elegant interior was dismantled and then rebuilt piece by piece in the new Lyric Theatre in the middle of the shopping mall and office buildings. The Mall and Lyric Theatre have just undergone some more work, with the scaffolding coming down just as we went to press.

As part of the local summer festival, a big screen was erected in the Square. People could watch some of our big sporting events like Wimbledon from the comfort of some handily provided deck chairs.

King Street

This Page: Running off of King Street, Macbeth Street and Nigel Playfair Avenue both feature fabulous displays of spring blossom. The avenue was named after a playwright of the same name, who lived in the area and whose production of Shakespeare's *As You Like It* was considered groundbreaking for theatre.

Nigel Playfair Avenue runs alongside the impressive council buildings, which at the A4 end have some steps, bordered by these magnificent sculptures of Old Father Thames (below). If you would like to know more about these structures and much more you might like to follow the work of The Hammersmith and Fulham Historic Buildngs Group *www.hfhbg.org.uk* – amongst much campaigning, one of their early successes was to save Bradmore House from destruction (see page 53).

Opposite: Cambridge Grove gives easy access from King Street to Glenthorne Road, and runs under the green railway bridge. The railings seen in the picture have been there since 1869, spared from melting down in WWII out of fear for public safety during a black out. This street was featured in the 1952 film *Cosh Boys*.

Until the 18th century, King Street, the main shopping street of Hammersmith, was known as Brentford Road. A bomb crater in the road during the last war lead to the one way traffic system which continues to this day.

Top left: The Hop Poles has, in its time, been a hotel as well as a pub. It was interesting to discover that in the early 1800s there were apparently as many as 37 public houses in Hammersmith, with astonishingly three called The Hop Poles, which must have made it very confusing. Thanks to the Independent R's website for these most illuminating facts *www.indyrs.co.uk*

Bottom left: Hammersmith Cineworld on King Street was designed by William R. Glen in 1936. It was initially called the Regal cinema, and opened with the Clark Gable film, 'Wife vs Secretary'.

Top right: A plant bed outside the Hammersmith and Fulham Council Town Hall spells out their initials in flowers.

Opposite: Home to over 40 shops, Kings Mall shopping centre has everything that you might need in one place. It was refurbished and extended in 2013, and its sleek, white new interiors really reflect the modernity of the city.

Bottom left:
The Salutation Pub

Inset: A plaque just inside the door of The Salutation tells you the history of their name: Lieutenant Lapenotiere galloped by on his historic route from Falmouth to the Admiralty in Whitehall carrying dispatches with the news of the Battle of Trafalgar. It also commemorates the local men who fought alongside Lord Nelson.

St Peter's Square

The architectural historian Nikolaus Pevsner wrote that St Peter's Church was "cheaply built and shabby" but this was felt by many to be an unfair description of such a delightful building; its Grecian style edifice was built more as an amenity to attract residents to the area, rather than to serve an existing population. George Scott, who donated the land on which it is built, wanted it to be named St George but when it was consecrated in 1829 Saint Peter won the day.

The 43 houses in St Peter's Square, dating from the 1820s were built in sets of three and have the appearance of large detached villas, many of them still retaining their original lion, dog and eagle decorations – Numbers 1–6 were completed first (see picture overleaf) and are considered to be the finest. An engine house in the centre of the square originally supplied the houses with fresh water from a deep artesian well. Following a controversial plan to redevelop the square, it was purchased by the local council and opened as a public park in 1915.

Right: At the heart of the square is a beautiful garden, which is home to Sir William Blake Richmond's elegant statue of The Greek Runner. It is forever leaping through this delightful garden square. It was placed here in 1926 as a memorial to the local painter.

Below right: Just off the square the Carpenters Arms was given a 5 star review for their excellent food, but in a bizarre twist of events, this turned out to be a bad thing. So inundated with bookings, it turned from being a friendly local pub to an upmarket restaurant. The efforts of the owners have returned the pub to its former welcoming atmosphere, back to being a weekly haunt for locals, rather than a monthly treat.

The River and
Upper & Lower Mall

Starting at the end of Chiswick Mall, Hammersmith Upper and Lower Mall stretches along the river to meet Hammersmith Bridge. In the past, sailing up the Thames was considered the safest method of travel for royalty on their journeys from Richmond and Hampton Court palaces, and Windsor Castle, rather than the dangerous roads. This half mile stretch of the river has five pubs enjoying views across the river, including the Black Lion, with one of the few remaining skittle alleys in London, and the historic Dove. Many famous figures enjoyed a drink at the establishment; the patriotic Rule Britannia was composed overlooking the Thames by James Thompson. In 1900, Cobden Sanderson and Sir Emery Walker started the Dove Press next door, a partnership infamous for its destruction; Cobden Sanderson, so protective of The Doves Font that they had created together, "bequeathed" the typeface to the Thames, dumping over a ton of metal over the bridge to be lost forever. It is now available as a digital download. Also on the Mall, William Morris' old coach house, former meeting place for his Hammersmith Socialist League, is now a museum run by the William Morris Society who perpetuate the memory of one of the most celebrated men of the Victorian age.

Sometimes on a still night
the river can be beautifully
calm, until a boat comes
along, that is. Taken from
Hammersmith Bridge.

Fulham Reach's new pontoon
rests on the water as the sky
turns pink at dusk.

Top Left: Looking towards the pontoons of Upper Latymer and the Sailing Club.

The houseboats that form a floating community on the Mall in front of Furnivall Gardens point west towards Chiswick. It must be a wonderful place to live on a clear day like this.

Built for river steamers to journey to the Festival of Britain in 1951, the original ticket office on Dove Pier remains on one of the pontoons whilst residential moorings have created a village on the water.

Lower Mall has been home to many famous people over the centuries. George Devine, who founded the English Stage Company based at the Royal Court Theatre, lived at number 9 whilst Sir Stamford Raffles, founder of Singapore, was educated at a boys' school at Kent House. Until recent years Thames Watermen lived in the small cottages next to the Blue Anchor and offered skiffs for hire just west of Hammersmith Bridge.

Inset: A pair of Moorhens regularly nest in this tyre, attached to one of boats moored up beside The Mall, which is a bit precarious to say the least.

Above: The houseboats at low tide tilt on the bank among the seagulls on a misty day.

The same view along the river at very different times of day and year, one at dawn in late spring and the other one, a fine autumn afternoon.

The Mall, Hammersmith.

Opposite: A boat cuts through the still water to make waves across from Hammersmith Terrace and St Peter's church.

Top left: This card depicting Lower Mall was posted in Barnes on May 3rd 1912. Image courtesy of Chris Bond.

Top right: The low tide in the summer at Lower Mall transforms the river into a beach. Maybe if you look hard, you might be able to find the long lost Doves typeface, thrown off the bridge in 1916 by T. J. Cobden-Sanderson.

Once warehouses occupied this lovely stretch of Hammersmith's river, serving the boats which ferried produce to and from the market gardens and nurseries.

The Lower Mall is a wonderful place to enjoy yourself on a warm summer's evening, with all the pubs being very popular and the umbrellas being used for shade rather than from the rain.

There are plenty of pubs along the Mall for hot summer days. Opposite is the view up the river from the Rutland Arms as the summer sun bathes the Lower Mall, or the Blue Anchor can provide a cold beer for the evening.

Rutland Arms: Another long standing Hammersmith riverside pub beloved over the years by the oarsmen of local rowing clubs. Why it has the name of the smallest historic county in England is lost in the mists of time but the inn's sign of Rutland's coat of arms with motto *Multum in Parvo* – Much in Little – is certainly a good description of a beer glowing in the bottom of a glass after a walk beside the river on a summer's day.

Opposite: The view west from outside the Blue Anchor.

Below: The Blue Anchor can trace its roots back to 1722, when licensing began in the area, and was the only pub to be listed, making it one of the oldest pubs in Hammersmith. For centuries it was a favourite haunt of the Watermen who lived in nearby cottages. Next door the Rutland Arms, built in the 1870s, flies the flags for the World Cup.

Opposite: Furnivall Sculling Club is just two doors from Furnivall Gardens, both named after the charitable Victorian Dr Furnivall, who started the club.

Many actors, artists, politicians, writers and nobility have raised a glass in the historic Dove pub, originally an 18th century coffee house. Sir Alan Herbert, a local resident, featured the pub in his popular novel, The Water Gipsies, where it appears as 'The Pigeons'. The establishment claims that King Charles II seduced his mistress Nell Gwyne here, and that James Thompson composed Rule Brittania in the pub. One certifiable claim to fame is that, according to Guinness World Records, it has the smallest bar room in the world, just on your right as you enter the pub.

Queen Catherine of Braganza, widow of Charles II, lived on Upper Mall for several years in Rivercourt, a grand mansion, and planted a row of elms overlooking the river which until the 1930s were referred to as 'Braganzas'. They eventually succumbed to elm disease and the last was felled in 1954.

This Page: Saved from demolition due to is important landing stage when the adjacent West Middlesex Water Works were built in the early 19th century, for years The Old Ship remained sandwiched between the noise and pollution of heavy industry. Now that the factories have gone and its entrance moved to the riverside, customers enjoy an unrivalled view of the Thames and open garden space.

Opposite: Built on a former piggery, over the last couple of centuries the Black Lion has been a popular drinking place for local artists and writers as well as workers from the nearby bakery and water works. The pub is notorious for its association with the Hammersmith Ghost, though when Francis Smith lay in wait with his gun in 1804, he found after he had shot the apparition that the 'ghost' was in fact a bricklayer. Smith was sentenced to be hanged for murder but happily received a royal pardon. It also houses the last remaining skittle alley in London.

Opposite bottom right: Continuing the walk along the Thames, you find Hammersmith Terrace, a set of houses originally designed as affordable accommodation, all with an impressive set of pillars outside their front doors. Number 7 is the former home of English painter and engraver Emery Walker, and it now stands as a museum, preserved by his daughter. It is furnished in the style of the Arts and Crafts movement, and contains many of William Morris' personal effect in the house, as he was a founder of the movement.

Ravenscourt Park

This page top left: The grand five story Ravenscourt Hospital, also known as the Royal Masonic Hospital, opened in 1933 as a private hospital. Having closed down in 2006, part of the building has since re-opened as a specialist hospital whilst the iconic nurses home is now apartments.

The red brick houses with white trim around the doors and windows in Hamlet Gardens are beautiful to behold. A factory used to be in this area, but the buildings and the garden square has since become solely residential.

The delightful little Westcroft Square stands on land that was originally property of Palingswick Manor, but in the 1830s residential building began, and since the flats were built in the 1890s, the square has not changed much in the last century. The open square is a beautiful public space for the houses and for any travelers passing through — or a cat.

Bottom left: This lovely building on the Dalling Road started life as a dance hall, before being transformed into the Ebenezer Chapel by the Albion Congregational Church, eventually becoming home to the Salvation Army which had been founded by local resident William Booth.

Top and bottom right: Dorville Crescent

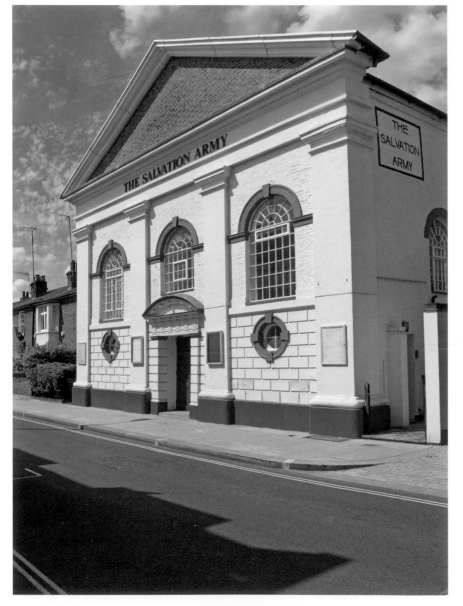

This page: You may be interested to know that Ravenscourt Park tube station was built on the site of a former lepper hospital – the last occupant moved out in the 1600s.

The London Blacksmith
Tel: 0203 701 8523

Opposite: For seventy years Queen Charlotte's Hospital was known as the baby hospital and thousands of mothers gave birth there. During the labour, husbands retreated to the Raven in Goldhawk Road for a stiff drink, and to sign the book kept by the publican for proud fathers to record the family's achievement. The hospital has moved but the original Gothic Oakbrook Lodge, first a nurses' home and then the Hospital's finance department, has survived and is now elegant apartments.

This page: The corner of Ravenscourt Square and Goldhawk Road has long said goodbye to its laundries and dairies although a 1930s garage facade still remains. However, it is nice to see that some of the old traders are making a comeback in this part of town. Peer over the stable door and watch carpenter Joshua Tait creating furniture and cupboards whilst 'The London Blacksmith' next door, Will Barker, makes sparks fly from his forge. He has been here for over a year, though has been a smithy for over ten years. Around the corner is a vintage textile shop, a retailer of exclusive children's clothes and a specialist in bespoke handmade hardwood floors. The Jag Shop supplies parts worldwide and splendid vintage Jaguars can be admired at the repair shop at the rear. A truly artisan corner.

Brackenbury

This spread: Wingate Road is known for its colour coordinated houses.

Opposite top right: This striking building is actually so big that it has faces on both Tabor Road and Iffley Road! Built in 1886, before the rest of the road, this was originally St John's Church, but since 1970 it has been used as an artist's studio.

Left: Telephone lines cross the sky in the picturesque Cardross Street.

Top right: On account of peoples wish to know more about what they eat, local shops are making a comeback, none more so than your family butchers. John Stenton Family Butchers on Aldensley Road is a traditional English and French butchery in the heart of Brackenbury Village.

The houses in Carthew
Road and in some of
the surrounding roads
display some particularly
fine tiles, which thankfully
most owners have made a
point of retaining.

Hammersmith Grove

This Spread: In 1880 George Wimpey established a stone yard in Hammersmith Grove. The company built the first Hammersmith Town Hall and the 80,000 seat stadium for the 1908 Olympic Games in nearby Shepherds Bush. His headquarters remained in Hammersmith Grove until recent years.

Opposite bottom right and below: The Grove Bar and Restaurant used to be a hotel back in the late 1800s with its latest incarnation opening in 1996.

Below top and bottom: the rather striking office building found half way down the Grove.

Left: Many pubs in the area display a wonderful array of hanging baskets outside their premises and the ones outside The Andover Arms in Aldensley Road are particularly fine.

Bottom: Tucked away in Brackenbury village, this popular Victorian pub was, to the relief of regulars, re-opened under new management in June 2014. Local actor James Purefoy tweeted at the news "The world is saved, the world is saved!"

Opposite: The Stonemasons Arms on the corner of Cambridge Grove and Glenthorne Road lies just opposite what used to be St John's Church, and is now a splendid new performing arts centre for Godolphin and Latymer School in Iffley Road.

Brook Green area

Opposite: Trussley Road is a very popular cut through, joining Brackenbury with Brook Green.

Top: Trussley Road is where some local businesses, including a supporter of this book, Shoots & Leaves, have made use of a popular form of premises, the railway arches.

Bottom right: Grove Mews off Trussley Road.

Loris Road

This spread: Tucked away on a small side street in Brook Green is a beautiful little town garden. Back in the long days of summer, the owner Cordelia very kindly showed me around. Built by local garden company, Shoots & Leaves, Cordelia is really pleased with how it has grown up and she says it's like passing into another world, leaving Brook Green at her front door, and moving through to the peace and tranquillity of her garden. She even had Shoots & Leaves put in a pizza oven, much loved by her children.

This page: Don't worry, you aren't seeing in triplicate; walking up Shepherds Bush Road, just past the Green, there really are three Holloways of Ludlow showrooms! Originally a salvage company, Mark Holloway has grown the business to include lighting, bathrooms, kitchens, interior design and general building.

Opposite top left: Loris Garden is a very sweet green space with a children's play area, a mosaic, grassy hills, and even a small pond. It relies on being maintained via public drop in days.

Opposite top right and bottom right: Luxemburg Gardens off Brook Green is considered one of the more sought after roads in the area, with its views across St Paul's Girls School playing fields.

Opposite bottom left: Based in the Victorian greenhouses (see page 164) in Ravenscourt Park, Hammersmith Community Gardens Association is a local environment charity, partly sponsored by this books main sponsor, Finlay Brewer, and for over 30 years have managed four community gardens in Hammersmith and Fulham.

To celebrate its 30th birthday they held a special day and put up this plaque in Loris Gardens.

Left: In the spring, Masbro Road is lit up with blossoming trees, the pink beautifully complimenting the blue of the Havelock Tavern which opened in 1996 and has changed very little since, boasting a casual relaxed atmosphere for its patrons.

Bottom left: Faroe Road

Bottom right: These white houses give Haarlem Road, running parallel to Brook Green, a very European feel.

Opposite top: The multicoloured buildings along Addison Gardens add a touch of colour to the street.

Opposite bottom: A flower pot in one of the windows in Girdlers Road sweetens the white flowered curtains.

Top left and opposite: Blythe Road in east Hammersmith is mainly a residential road, but it is also home to the grand Blythe House. Now an archive and store house for the major London museums, it opened in 1903 as the headquarters for the Post Office Savings Bank where over 4,000 staff handled more than 100,000 letters every day. Whilst the men used the main entrance the 1,000 women employees were segregated to the south block which had its own entrance.

The satellite dishes may proliferate but another sign of the times is the loss each week across the country of traditional pubs, with Brook Green not being immune, the Old Parrs Head on the end of this block in Blythe Road going in the summer 2014.

Bottom: This housing estate in Blythe Road sports classic art deco architecture.

Top and bottom right: Betty Blythe's Vintage Tea Room in Blythe Road is a rather tasty confection; fabulous decor based around the rather racy silent movie star Betty Blythe, combined with everything you'd expect of a traditional tea room. Thank you to Hannah, pictured behind her cakes, for letting me know something of the background and I very much look forward to coming back and tasting tea for real.

Wild Food Market

Held every Saturday in the grounds of Addison Primary School, the Wild Food Market, which started in the spring of 2014 and is run by Push (pictured bottom right), sells organic and locally sourced food to the local area. It holds classes to teach the community how to cook food from fresh, encouraging people to eat healthier.

Addison Primary School, just off Brook Green, caters for children aged 3–11 and occupies an old Victorian site with some noticeable modern additions.

Shepherds Bush Road

Opposite and top right: Statues of Shakespeare and Milton look down on Shepherds Bush Road passers-by from the splendid Hammersmith library built in 1905 by Henry Hare. Lavishly decorated with allegorical sculpture, it is interesting to note that whilst art, literature and craft are depicted by females, only science with a pair of dividers is portrayed as a male.

Right: Opposite the library a development is taking place, room by room.

Bottom right: Now Wagamama, the old firestation has been refurbished to accommodate a restaurant while still keeping the recognisable facade.

Opposite: The Laurie Arms on Shepherds Bush Road is a little glimpse of the past, tucked between the white modern buildings surrounding it. While it used to be a one room Irish pub, it has expanded with the conservatory next door.

Top left: Our sponsor, Finlay Brewer is the foremost independent estate agent in the area and has been in Brook Green for over 20 years.

Top right: A bike advertising Street Eats, a local restaurant that strives to produce honest and simple world foods.

Bottom left: Brooks Counter and Table Deli serves fresh, homemade lunch for visitors to the area and busy workers alike.

Hammersmith Road

Founded in 1509 by Dean John Colet, a friend of Erasmus, St Paul's School moved from the shadows of St Paul's Cathedral to a large red-brick building designed by Alfred Waterhouse in Hammersmith in 1884. The list of past pupils include John Milton, Samuel Pepys and Bernard Montgomery who used the building as his HQ during the war for planning the D-Day landings. The school moved once again to the other side of the river in Barnes in 1963 and the building was torn down, though the High Master's House was fortunately preserved and is now the boutique St Paul's Hotel.

The delicious Melody restaurant in the hotel was named after a British film from 1971 that was partially filmed in the school.

This Page: The sleek glass front of the modern Novotel hotel brings the inner city into the borough.

Opposite: The new London buses travel through Hammersmith.

South of the Broadway & Fulham Palace Road

When walking down Fulham Palace Road you might notice the many references to distilling: The Distillery pub (top left), The Old Suffolk Punch in Distillery Lane (bottom left) and the main building for the brand new Fulham Reach development, Distillery Wharf (opposite). This is not by chance, as until the mid 20th Century there used to be one on this site. Interestingly, there are are a few drinks companies based around Hammersmith; must be a theme.

Right: The River Cafe along the Thames Path at Thames Wharf was started in 1987 by the renowned chef Rose Gray, who sadly died in 2010, and Ruth Rogers, who influenced a generation of chefs. It was here that Jamie Oliver was talent spotted.

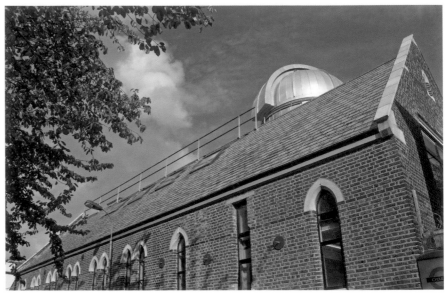

Opposite top left: The Chancellors pub in Crisp Road. The road was named after 17th century resident and friend of Charles I, Sir Nicholas Crisp.

Opposite top right: One of the larger buildings in Crisp Road, which is currently under development, looks to have its own large telescope on the roof.

Opposite bottom: Opposite the Guinness House Trust building on Fulham Place Road is the Peabody Estate. Started by Victorian businessman and philanthropist, George Peabody, the Peabody Trust, which aims to provide decent and affordable housing to the poor. This Hammersmith estate was opened in 1926 and covers almost six acres of land. It was bought from a convent, and the nuns burial ground is now a sunken lawn, pictured.

Top: The Guinness Trust Foundation Charity houses provide affordable living for the capitals homeless.

Bottom: This view down the Thames shows the Old Harrods Depository on the left, Harrods Village, and on the near right, the curved roof of the offices of Sir Richard Rogers, the world renowned architect.

Schools

St Paul's Girls School: Founded by the Mercers in 1889 to complement the nearby boys' school, the graceful Victorian main building is on the site of former almshouses and the grounds of The Grange, former home of the actor Henry Irving. The school certainly benefitted musically having Gustav Holst followed by Herbert Howells as directors of music. Holst composed his St Paul's and Brook Green suites especially for the pupils.

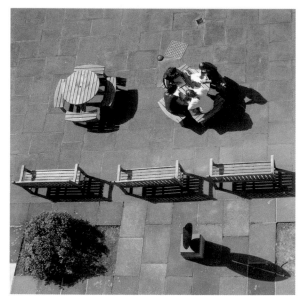

Godolphin and Latymer School: Tucked behind busy King Street, on Iffley Road, is Godolphin and Latymer School, which my own daughter attended up until 2012. Starting as Godolphin School in 1861, a boarding establishment for boys and set in fields just by the river in Hammersmith, in 1905 it became an independent day school for girls, associated with the Latymer Foundation and taking the name of the Godolphin and Latymer School.

Upper Latymer: Founded by a bequest of Edward Latymer in 1624 to provide "eight poore boies" with a doublet, a pair of breeches, shirt, pair of woollen stockings as well as some education, Latymer Upper School now occupies a prestigous site on King Street. With a boat house by the river, it is not surprising that Upper Latymer is in the forefront of school rowing.

Founded in 1991, Ravenscourt Park Prep School is one of the newest educational establishments in this area of London. This co-educational school has a fine record.

As with Godolphin, I am particularly fond of this place, as both my children went to school here and although the grounds have expanded massively since they left eight years ago, it's nice to find that nothing else has changed, down to the delightful Mrs Taylor still looking after reception.

Thanks to the manager of Premier Inn across the street for letting me photograph from the top floor!

Brackenbury Primary School: When visiting the red brick Brackenbury Primary School in North Hammersmith, visitors should take note of the old doorway for girls and infants, a relic of times gone by. A newer addition to the school is the library, with illustrations of the Gruffalo by Julia Donaldson on the walls, and was opened by the writer and illustrator herself.

Opposite: Bute House girls school was built in 1958 on the former grounds of a Victory Garden during the World Wars. The school crest features a birch tree that survived the Blitz, though has since been felled due to a fungal infection, and a new tree has been grown in its place.

This page: In 1859 Dr. John Betts, a local medical practitioner and landowner, created a trust in order that "a good substantial schoolhouse of brick and stone" should be built on a piece of land in Albion (now Paddenswick) Road. The first pupils – 142 boys, 115 girls and 85 infants – were enrolled in 1871.

Open Spaces

Part of what makes London such a beautiful city are its green open spaces, always available for a weary commuter in need of a breath of fresh air. Hammersmith has its fair share of parks, each beautifully kept and in easy walking distance of the town centre. Ravenscourt Park begins at the west end of Hammersmith, and is the largest of our parks. This park was once the site of Palingswick Manor, later named Ravenscourt, but it was demolished after being bombed in WWII. Features of the manor still remain; the Tea House on the east side of park used to be the Stable Block, and the lake at the top of the park is the remains of a moat. Not all of the parks features are ancient, however; aside from a children's playpark with an open air paddling pool, in the Summer many events are held, including film screenings on the lawn. On the Upper Mall, on the former site of an industrial estate, before it was bombed in the blitz, Furnivall Gardens has a beautiful riverside view, a very short stroll from the Dove pub. With Brook Green, Margravine Cemetery, and the scattered garden squares like St Peter's Square, this area is lucky to have such a rich array of beautiful open spaces.

Ravenscourt Park

Opposite bottom right: A memorial to Giles Hart stands in the park. Among his many achievements, he was chairman, secretary and treasurer of the Polish Solidarity Campaign, but died in the 7/7 London bombings.

A public park since 1888, traces of the original Tudor house still lie beneath the grass. The most notorious occupant of Pallingswick Manor, the original name of the 14th century moated manor, was Alice Perrers, the mistress of Edward III. The house had its own chapel and bake house and was surrounded by over 100 acres of arable land through which flowed a tributary of the Stamford Brook.

The estate was later owned by Thomas Corbett, who in 1746 changed its name to Ravenscourt, his coat of arms shows "a raven sable with many quarterings" – the French for raven is corbeau.

This page: Far from being just a beautiful space, Ravenscourt Park has four playgrounds for the children, though the grown-ups have been spotted enjoying the rope slide. It also has tennis and basket ball courts.

While this serene bench between the trees remains unchanged all year round, the park changes around it.

The park offers all comers the chance to enjoy some peace, from mothers with prams, to the many people exercising their dogs to joggers.

Top: The steeple of Rivercourt Methodist Church can be seen rising above the trees on the South of the park, one of the few buildings outside the park visible from within.

Bottom Left: The moat from Palingswick Manor can still be found in the form of the lake in the centre of the park.

The walled garden: Originally the vegetable garden for Ravenscourt House, the walled garden has a splendid Armillary sundial which was presented by the Friends of the Walled Garden to mark the 125th anniversary of the opening of the park on 19th May 1888.

To find out more about the work of the Friends please visit *www.ravenscourtgarden.btck.co.uk*

Top right: These community garden greenhouses can be found behind the cafe (opposite) and are run by Hammersmith Community Gardens Association (see page 119), one of the many organisations our sponsor, Finlay Brewer, supports. They can be found at *hcga.org.uk*

Opposite: The old Stable House of the manor is now used as a cafe for visitors to the park.

What better way to cool off in the long, hot summer days spent in the park than the children's paddling pool just beneath the railway line. Kids and parents can take a splash to cool off.

Just under the bridge on Ravenscourt Avenue out of the park lies the little gem that is the West Six Garden Centre, which caters for both the keen gardener with its large selection of flowers, trees and shrubs, to the more casual buyer, with its well stocked gift shop.

Thanks to Louise and Joel for letting me take these pictures.

Furnivall Gardens

Opposite bottom left: the Town Hall can be seen on the other side of the gardens.

Until 1929 Thames Watermen negotiated their barges up the Creek, the mouth of the ancient waterway of Stamford Brook. The Creek was a magnet for fishermen and traders including the Hammersmith Brewery, builders Sankey and Clark's Lead Mills. The Creek was culverted in 1936 and still runs under Hammersmith Town Hall. A flying bomb destroyed most of the lead mills in 1944 and Furnivall Gardens was opened in 1951. Despite the endless traffic travelling on the Great West Road, Furnivall Gardens continues to give the area a sense of space and calm and keep the river sacred.

Margravine Cemetery

This pleasant open space in a heavily built-up area was formerly Hammersmith's cemetery, opening in 1869 following an outbreak of cholera in the area. Ten acres of former market gardens and orchards were transformed into a burial ground with the larger part consecrated for Anglicans and the lesser un-consecrated for the nonconformists. The cemetery was bombed three times during the Second World War and subsequently in 1951 became a Garden of Rest.

The cemetery is just next door to the threatened Charing Cross Hospital. Opened by Dr. Benjamin Golding in 1818, it was a dream of his to establish a place to heal the poor. The hospital moved here in 1973, but it is now under threat from budget cuts, and may have the A&E and Stroke Unit closed.

There are not only humans at risk from this closure – a pair of Peregrines nest on the roof named Charlie and Tom. First spotted in October 2007, avid watcher Nathalie has been blogging about them ever since. You can even follow Tom and Charlie (inset left) on Twitter, and via a webcam that has been set up.

Frank Banfield Park was created in the 1970s following the housing clearance of Elmdale and Playfair Streets in 1974. Banfield himself was the local Mayor and Alderman of Fulham but died in 1970 after a lifetime of public service. This small park on the south of Hammersmith is perfect for a picnic or a breath of fresh air on a long day.

On the River

As Hammersmith is so well situated on the Thames, it's no surprise that water-sports are such a well-loved activity in the area, making full use of the Thames on its doorstep with rowing and sailing. In opposition to the elitism present in the Amateur Rowing Association at the time, Dr Frederick James Furnivall, co-creator of the Oxford English Dictionary, founded the Hammersmith Sculling Club for girls, in an effort to encourage more women to join in the sport. In 1901 the club was opened to men but the captaincy remained restricted to female members for the first half of the century. Dr Furnivall's many good deeds included opening a school for poor men and boys and selling his book collection to donate to support striking woodcutters. The renamed Furnivall Sculling Club remains on the Lower Mall, open for anyone to join.

After their club house near Hammersmith Bridge was bombed in 1944, the Corinthian Sailing Club relocated to Linden House (see overleaf) which it shares with Sons of the Thames Rowing Club. Former members include Sir Roger Bannister, broadcaster Dr. Magnus Pyke and naturalist Sir Peter Scott.

Strand on the Green Sailing club regularly sail up to
Hammersmith from their club. Here, on the last race outing of
the year in November 2013, it actually wasn't that cold – it was
a beautiful sunny autumn day. I followed them back up river on
their return to Strand on the Green and they all struggled given
there was absolutely no wind to help them.

Thanks to Chris Greenwood for informing me about the club.

Rowing is a sport for all
weathers and conditions but
at dusk on a high tide they
can make the perfect picture
(see overleaf).

The combination of the sun on the Thames can provide some spectacular scenes.

Local walks
HOW TO TRULY EXPERIENCE
HAMMERSMITH & BROOK GREEN

We felt it would be nice to incorporate a couple of walks so that you can truly experience the beauty of the area for yourself. Here you will find details on two of the many walks around the area. The maps can also be found on the dust jacket of this book. A full detailed guide to the walks can be found on either of the following websites to be downloaded as an A4 sheet: *www.unity-publishing.co.uk www.finlaybrewer.co.uk*. Both these walks have been compiled for us by Caroline MacMillan, and you can either choose to complete the walks yourselves or to go with Caroline, who will be very pleased to guide you around. We can only fit so much on our walk sheet, so if you were to go with Caroline you would learn a lot more: *www.westlondonwalks.co.uk*. In addition to these walks she also conducts several others.

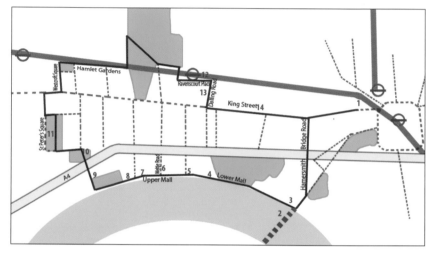

Our first walk is set in the south west part of the borough, following the river along Lower and Upper Mall before travelling north to reach Ravenscourt Park, and then along the bustling King Street to get back to the station. On this journey you will see a collection of Hammersmith's green spaces, with Furnivall Gardens and Upper Mall open space both on the Thames with beautiful riverside views, and North Verbena Garden, St Peter's Square, Westcroft Gardens and Ravenscourt Park all tucked between the houses. Several historic pubs are along this route; the Dove, with the smallest bar room in London, The haunted Black Lion, and The Salutation on King Street. On this short walk you can get to know the borough a little bit better, discover gardens you didn't know existed, and see the town in a new light.

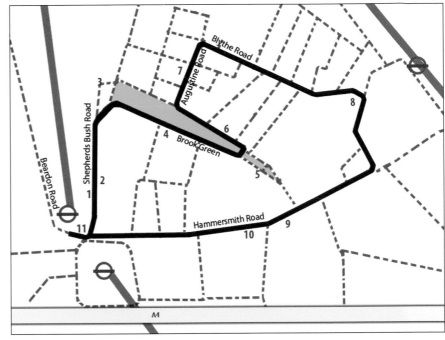

Our second walk takes you around the delightful Brook Green, blessed with beautiful houses, churches, historic buildings and a real community driven atmosphere. While it's not far from the busy town centre, with the concrete flyover, the 'New French Quarter' feels a world away. On this route, you will travel from the Broadway north up Shepherds Bush Road, seeing the old Fire Station and the Library, before taking a stroll along the green. You will pass the old Queen's Head, a number of blue plaque houses, before heading towards Blythe Road. The magnificent old Blythe House, the former post office, still stands, leading you back to Hammersmith Road.

This Page: From the top, Brook Green, St Paul's Girls School, The Osram Building and Holy Trinity Church.

Thank you to Teresa Brewer, Simon Gresswell, Paul Cosgrove and all the staff at Finlay Brewer Estate Agents for their kind support of my book.

020 7371 4171

info@finlaybrewer.co.uk

Finlay Brewer
138 Shepherds Bush Road
London W6 7PB

First Edition – © Unity Print and Publishing Limited 2014

Designed by Ball Design Consultancy
www.balldesignconsultancy.com

Printed by Page Brothers of Norwich, Norfolk.
www.pagebros.co.uk

Colour Management by Paul Sherfield of The Missing Horse Consultancy.
www.missinghorsecons.co.uk

Publishing Assistant: Jessica Dean

Published by Unity Print and Publishing Limited,
18 Dungarvan Avenue,
London SW15 5QU.
Tel: +44 (0)20 8487 2199
aw@unity-publishing.co.uk
www.unity-publishing.co.uk

Thank you to Hew Stevenson and all the staff at Shoots & Leaves for their kind support of my book.

Shoots & Leaves
Landscape Design & Construction

The Railway Arches, 235 Trussley Road, London W6 7PP
Tel: 0208 563 7733   Email: hew@shootsandleaves.co.uk

HOLLOWAYS of LUDLOW

Thank you to Mark Holloway and all the staff at Holloways of Ludlow for their kind support of my book.

020 7602 5757

sales@hollowaysofludlow.com

121 Shepherds Bush Road, Brook Green, Hammersmith, London W6 7LP

Follow Andrew on Twitter:
@andrewpics

Inhabitons

Green

The Creek

PADDING WICK

GREEN

Four Miles from Hyde Park Corner

THAME

CHISWICK

HAM

The Bowling Alley